Soccer Superstar

Phil Kettle
illustrated by Craig Smith

Distributed in
the United States of America
by Pacific Learning
P.O. Box 2723
Huntington Beach, CA
92647-0723

Website:
www.pacificlearning.com

Published by Black Hills
(an imprint of Toocool Rules
Pty Ltd)
PO Box 2073
Fitzroy MDC VIC 3065
Australia
61+3+9419-9406

First published in the United States by Black Hills in 2004.
American editorial by Pacific Learning in 2004.
Text copyright © Phillip Kettle, 2002.
Illustration copyright © Toocool Rules Pty Limited, 2002.

 a black dog and Springhill book

Printed in China through Colorcraft Ltd, Hong Kong

ISBN 1 920924 12 4
PL-6212

10 9 8 7 6 5 4 3 2 1   08 07 06 05 04

Contents

Mr. Lopez

Marcy

Roberto

Gemma

Tony

Simon

Dan

Eddie

Dog

Toocool

Chapter 1
The Meeting

On Saturday morning, I called an urgent meeting. Some kids from a nearby town wanted to play a game of soccer against us. The game would be played in Toocool Park.

We had a week to get ready.

Marcy said she would be captain. I thought I should be captain, but I kept my mouth shut. I didn't want to upset Marcy. She's almost as good at soccer as I am.

Eddie was in a hurry—he wanted to get some lunch. He agreed to play any position.

Dan was nervous. He said we needed more practice. Roberto said Dan was a worrywart. Roberto said legends are always ready to play.

Simon put extra oil on his wheels. He was ready for the game of his life.

That left Dog. All he wanted to do was run around and sniff the trees. He wouldn't be much help.

Our team is called the Legends.

The other team call themselves the Westside Winners. We call them the Westside Whiners.

Kickoff was at ten o'clock the next Saturday morning. All we needed was a coach.

Chapter 2
The Coach

Mr. Lopez said he would be happy to coach us. He said he would teach us a thing or two. We weren't interested in a thing or two—whatever that meant. We just wanted him to teach us about soccer.

Every day after school,
Mr. Lopez was waiting for us.
He always wore his special
coaching T-shirt.

Eddie hated practicing. He said he never had time to eat. Marcy told him to stop complaining and start running. She loved practicing. She was really excited.

"I'm going to squash them like lemons!" she yelled.

I was glad it was them and not me.

I practiced the hardest. I
sprinted up and down TC Park.
I dribbled the ball until I was
in professional form. I practiced
kicking and heading.

Roberto was getting faster.
He'd be able to dodge any
player on the other team. Simon
had all the right moves. Even
Dan's game was getting better.

Mr. Lopez was a tough coach, but he was good.

I was sure everyone on our team would soon be a soccer superstar like I was.

Mr. Lopez had other ideas.

Chapter 3
Kicking Practice

Mr. Lopez said we were terrible kickers. He said if you can't kick, you can't make goals. It was time to practice taking shots on goal.

Marcy went first.
She slammed the ball at the
goal. It was a great shot. Then
suddenly, Dog came out of
nowhere! He leaped through the
air. He knocked the ball out of
the goal and chased it away.

We all tried, but even I
couldn't get the ball past Dog.

Mr. Lopez called us over.

"How can you win if you can't even get the ball past Dog?" he said. "Give me the ball. I'll show you how the pros do it."

We all stood back. This was going to be interesting.

"Watch closely," he said.

He moved in slowly, brought his leg back, and kicked.

It was a fantastic kick! Even Mr. Lopez looked surprised. Dog's head was spinning as the ball flew past him.

"That's how you take a shot on goal!" Mr. Lopez shouted.

Everyone cheered.

"That's what you have to do on Saturday," he said.

The team looked worried.

Chapter 4

The Secret Weapon

Our supporters were the first to arrive at TC Park. Roberto's mom had a banner for us to burst through. Simon's dad handed out the team shirts. Eddie's dad gave us a big basket of food for later. Marcy's sister was the referee. Mom was the crowd controller. She's good at that.

The pressure was on.
I looked around for the TV cameras, but I couldn't see them. They were probably hidden in the trees.

Mr. Lopez gave a talk on the three *P*s of soccer—pace, power, and pressure.

We weren't sure what he was talking about, but it sounded good.

Then the Westside Winners arrived. They looked mean. Mr. Lopez told us not to worry. He said our team had a secret weapon. I knew he was talking about me, but I didn't say anything.

"Our secret weapon," whispered Mr. Lopez, "is Dog. He's our goalie. They'll never get the ball past him."

We burst through the banner, and the crowd cheered. The Westside Winners laughed.

"Can you believe they have a dog on their team?" they yelled. "Woof, woof. Get ready to lose!"

"Just ignore them!" called Mr. Lopez. "Remember, we have a secret weapon."

No one scored in the first half. The ball just went up and down the field.

Then, in the second half, I set up the perfect goal.

I passed the ball to Simon. Simon slammed the ball to Eddie. Eddie dropped his cake and passed the ball to Roberto. Roberto dribbled around the Winners. He took a shot on goal, but he didn't kick hard enough.

Marcy sprinted from the middle of the field. She screamed at the Winners, "Get out of my way, or I'll squash you all like lemons!"

The Winners jumped out of her way.

She raced forward with the ball.

21

I'm sure I saw smoke coming from the ball.

The goalie saw it, too. His knees started to shake. The ball was like a missile coming at him. He tried to dive for cover, but he was too slow. The ball knocked off his hat and flew into the net.

Marcy did three cartwheels.
We ran over and hugged her.
The Winners just stood
there. They had never seen
soccer superstars like us.

Chapter 5
The Last Minute

In the last minute of the game, the Winners brought on a new player. He was the biggest, meanest player we'd ever seen.

He ran right through us and blasted the ball at the goal.

Oh, no!

The crowd held its breath.

It was Dog to the rescue!
Dog flew through the air like a
superhero. He headed the ball
as hard as he could. The ball
bounced into the sky. It sailed
into the crowd and out
of bounds.

Our secret weapon worked! The Winners had lost their only chance to score.

Dog ran around the field barking. The crowd cheered. I was a legend, and now my dog was a legend, too!

The Westside Whiners got on their bikes. They said they were going home to check the rules. We already knew there was no rule that said you couldn't have a dog as your secret weapon.

The Winners said they
would be back, and next time
we'd better be scared. They said
they would beat us at baseball.
We said they could try!
The End!

Toocool's
Soccer Glossary

Dodge—To quickly move one way and then the other. You dodge when you don't want the people on the other team to catch you.

Dribble—To move the ball by kicking it along the ground by yourself.

Goalie—The player who has to try to keep the ball from going into the net. Each team has only one goalie.

Header—When a player uses his or her head to pass the ball to another player, or to take a shot on goal.

Toocool's Map
The Soccer Field

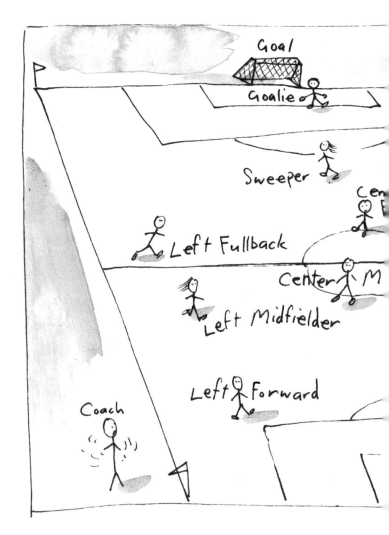

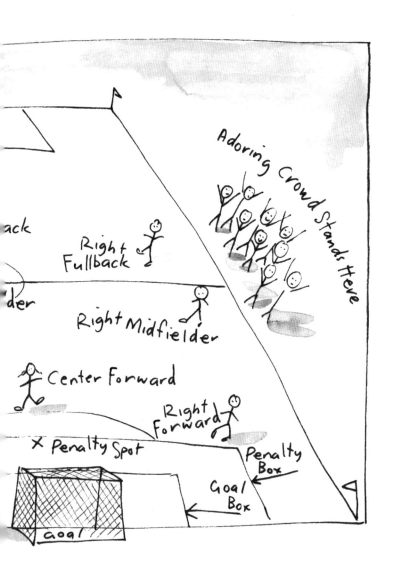

ack

Right
Fullback

der

Right Midfielder

Center Forward

Right
Forward

Adoring Crowd Stands Here

X Penalty Spot

Penalty
Box

Goal
Box

Goal

Toocool's Quick Summary
Soccer

Soccer is an incredibly popular sport. It is played in more countries than any other team sport. In some countries, soccer is called football.

The soccer field is shaped like a rectangle. At each end, there is a goal area with a net. You score a goal by kicking or heading the ball over your opponent's goal line and into the net.

A goal is worth one point.

Soccer teams have eleven players, but when you play with your friends, you don't have to stick to that rule. You can have as many players on your team as you want.

The only players who are allowed to touch the ball with their hands are the goalies. The other players use their feet to stop the ball and to kick it. If you're a superstar like I am, you can also use your head to pass the ball and to shoot on goal.

The Legends' Secret Weapon

The slow-motion replay

of the Secret Weapon

Q & A with Toocool
He Answers His Own Questions

🏐 **Why are you such a good soccer player?**

I find it hard to talk about myself, because I am so modest. Oh, did I mention that, out of all my friends, I am the best soccer player? I am a soccer superstar because I am so fast! I can move faster than the speed of light. If you have been to TC Park, you might have heard a strange buzzing sound—that was me going past.

What other skills do you need to be a soccer superstar?

To be a superstar, you have to be able to dribble, and I don't mean down your chin. To dribble, you move the ball down the field using your feet. I am really good at this. I can dribble and dodge at the same time. You need to be able to kick the ball straight and hard. I can make goals whenever I feel like it, but I like to give my friends a chance to score.

How do you learn to pass the ball with your head?

Heading a ball requires a special skill. I have plenty of special skills. My dad says having a hard head also helps.

🌐 What is the most important position on the field?

The position that I play—but every team also needs a good goalie. Scoring goals doesn't mean much if you let the other team score goals, too. Our team has the best goalie. Like all good goalies, he can fly through the air, catch the ball, or head it away from the goal. I taught him everything he knows.

🌐 Can teams send in substitutes during a game?

Yes, but I don't ever need a substitute because I am such a superstar. I'm in such awesome shape that I never need to rest, and I am too good to get hurt.

What is a yellow card?

The referee gave me a yellow card once, but it was a mistake. A yellow card is a warning. The referee warned me for playing rough, but it wasn't me, it was Marcy. Marcy is pretty tough. She even got a red card once, but it wasn't her fault. The referee got in her way. She was going so fast, she ran right into him. If you get a red card, you are removed from the game.

Do you have to practice much to be a good soccer player?

Because of my natural ability, I don't have to practice much. If you want to be a great player like I am, you need to practice a lot.

Soccer Quiz

How Much Do You Know about Soccer?

Q1 What shape is a soccer ball?

A. Oval. *B.* Round. *C.* Square.

Q2 What shape is a soccer field?

A. Oval. *B.* Square. *C.* Rectangle.

Q3 If you hold on to your opponent, what will the referee do?

A. Send you home. *B.* Make you do ten push-ups. *C.* Call a foul.

Q4 What happens if you are offside?

A. The other team gets a free kick. *B.* You get into trouble with your parents. *C.* You have a fight with your best friend.

Q5 How many goalies are there in a game of soccer?

A. Two. *B.* One. *C.* Three.

Q6 What does it mean if the referee shows you a yellow card?

A. You have scored a goal.

B. You have been warned.

C. You are invited to a party.

Q7 How many players are there on a soccer team?

A. Eleven. *B.* Seven. *C.* Five.

Q8 When are you given a goal kick?

A. When you have played well.
B. If the referee thinks it is your birthday. **C.** When the ball passes over the goal line but does not go into the net.

Q9 What is passing?
A. Better than flunking.
B. Running faster than anyone else on your team. **C.** Kicking the ball to one of your teammates.

Q10 Who should be captain of the U.S. Soccer Team?
A. Mr. Lopez. **B.** Toocool. **C.** Dog.

ANSWERS

🌀 *1* B. 🌀 *2* C. 🌀 *3* C.

🌀 *4* A. 🌀 *5* A. 🌀 *6* B.

🌀 *7* A. 🌀 *8* C. 🌀 *9* C.

🌀 *10* B.

If you got ten questions right, you could become your team's secret weapon. If you got more than five right, you still need serious coaching. If you got fewer than five right, you probably belong with the Westside Winners.

TOOCOOL

Baseball's Best

There's a showdown in TC Park. There are two teams, but only one star pitcher. Let's hope he listens to his captain.

Titles in the Toocool series